Morning News from the Fair

by Derek Scott
illustrated by Naomi Lewis

Harcourt
SCHOOL PUBLISHERS

Copyright © by Harcourt, Inc.

All rights reserved. No part of this publication may be reproduced or transmitted in any form or by any means, electronic or mechanical, including photocopy, recording, or any information storage and retrieval system, without permission in writing from the publisher.

Requests for permission to make copies of any part of the work should be addressed to School Permissions and Copyrights, Harcourt, Inc., 6277 Sea Harbor Drive, Orlando, Florida 32887-6777. Fax: 407-345-2418.

HARCOURT and the Harcourt Logo are trademarks of Harcourt, Inc., registered in the United States of America and/or other jurisdictions.

Printed in Mexico

ISBN 10: 0-15-350638-5
ISBN 13: 978-0-15-350638-3

Ordering Options
ISBN 10: 0-15-350599-0 (Grade 2 On-Level Collection)
ISBN 13: 978-0-15-350599-7 (Grade 2 On-Level Collection)
ISBN 10: 0-15-357819-X (package of 5)
ISBN 13: 978-0-15-357819-9 (package of 5)

If you have received these materials as examination copies free of charge, Harcourt School Publishers retains title to the materials and they may not be resold. Resale of examination copies is strictly prohibited and is illegal.

Possession of this publication in print format does not entitle users to convert this publication, or any portion of it, into electronic format.

1 2 3 4 5 6 7 8 9 10   050   15 14 13 12 11 10 09 08 07 06

Characters

Reporter 1
(Kate)

Reporter 2
(Mark)

Producer

Anchor 1
(Bob)

Anchor 2
(Sue)

Setting: The set of a television newsroom

Producer: Ready? Action!

Anchor 1: This is *Morning News*. I'm Bob, and this is Sue. This morning, we have a special news report from the Summer Fair.

4

Anchor 2: We have two reporters at the fair. First we will go to Kate.

Anchor 1: Good morning, Kate.

Reporter 1: Good morning. It's so exciting here!

Anchor 1: What is that behind you, Kate?

Reporter 1: That's the roller coaster. More than a hundred people have been for a ride already. The people on there now are really screaming! You might be able to hear them!

Anchor 2: You are right! I *can* hear them. What is that over to your left, Kate?

Reporter 1: That's a brand new ride. The eight chairs fly out and spin around at an amazing speed. I guess I won't be going on that because I would be too scared!

Anchor 1: *I'd* like that ride, but what about you, Sue?

Anchor 2: It's not for me, Bob. I think *you* need to go to the fair and prove that you are brave enough for that ride!

Anchor 1: Thank you, Kate, and now put us through to Mark. Good morning, Mark. You are at a different part of the fair.

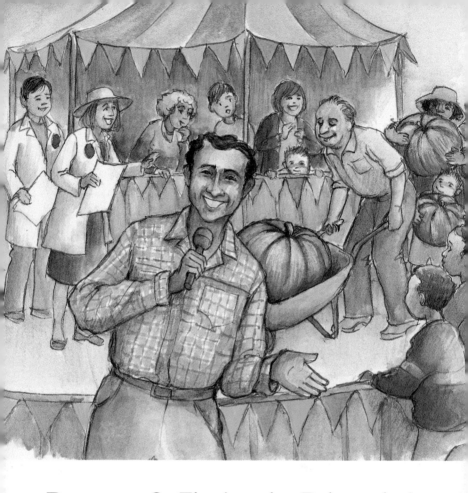

Reporter 2: That's right, Bob, and it's much quieter over here. Everything is ready for the biggest-pumpkin contest. Here comes the first pumpkin. Oh, sometimes I wonder just how big these pumpkins can get!

Anchor 1: I can see something else in the background. Can you tell us what is happening over there, Mark?

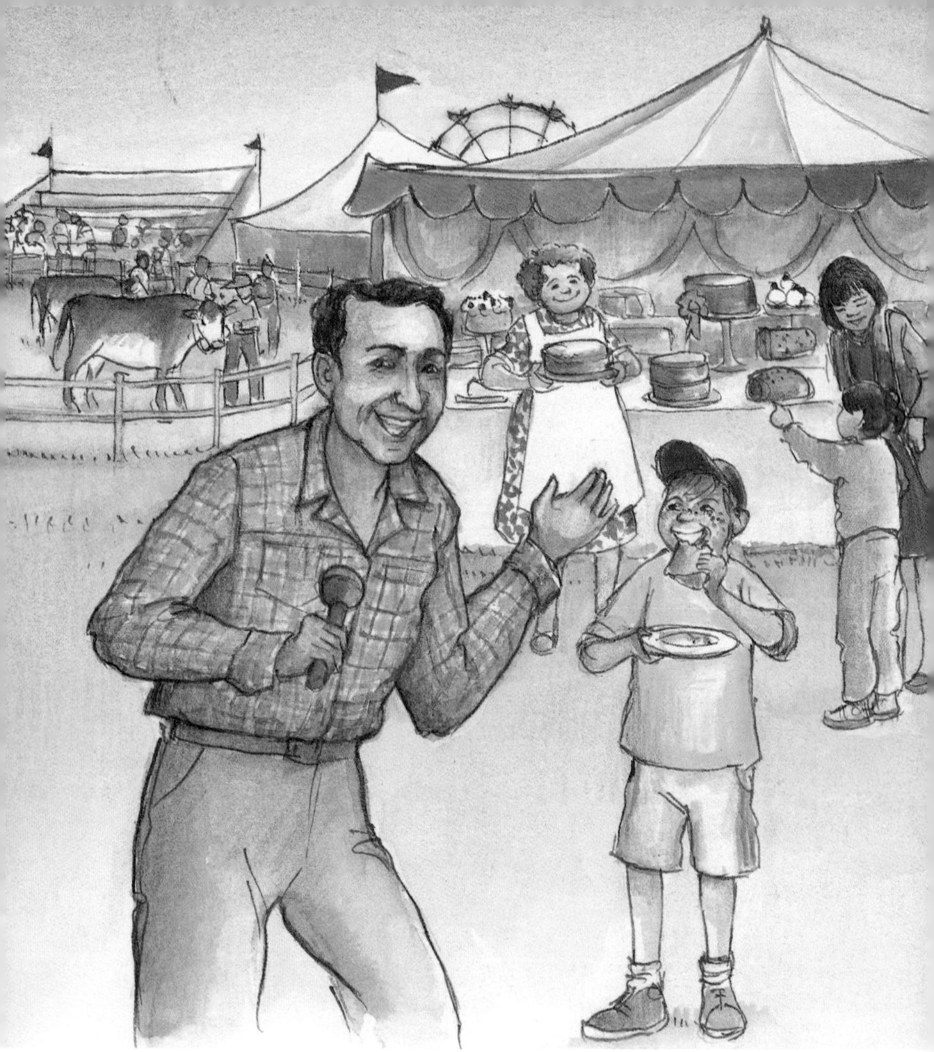

Reporter 2: That's where the cows are being shown. There is so much to see at this fair, Bob. Right now, I'm off to taste some carrot cakes!

Anchor 2: Finally, Mark, is there anything you would like to say to our viewers at home?

Reporter 2: I hope you will join us at the fair because we're having a great time!

Anchor 2: Thank you, Mark.

Anchor 1: That is *Morning News* for today. Don't miss the Summer Fair!

Producer: Well done! Thank you, team!

Think Critically

1. Where were the reporters and what were they talking about?

2. Which character do you think was in charge of the television newsroom? Why?

3. Why do you think people were screaming on the roller coaster?

4. What was the name of the news show?

5. What part of the Summer Fair would you like to see?

 **Social Studies**

Draw a Map Think about what you would like to see at a fair. Then make a map of the fair. Label your map.

School-Home Connection Talk about *Morning News from the Fair* with family members. Then ask them what news they have heard today.